MW00479592

Essential Question
How can starting a business help others?

START SMALL
THINK
BIG

BY
JULIA
WALL

Chapter 1

FROM SMALL BEGINNINGS

Starting a business takes time, energy, and courage. Every business begins with a great idea, but a great idea is not enough.

People who start businesses are called **entrepreneurs**. They work hard to make something that people will want to buy. Entrepreneurs have to convince people that their ideas are good. They need to find money to start their businesses.

Entrepreneurs often have setbacks. People may say their enterprises won't work. But when they succeed, entrepreneurs can make a big difference.

Lila and DeWitt Wallace took big risks to start a new business.

DeWitt and Lila Wallace decided to start a new magazine in 1919. DeWitt Wallace began a process of finding nonfiction articles that had been published. He made the articles shorter and put them into a magazine called *Reader's Digest*.

DeWitt Wallace sent 200 copies of the magazine to publishers. He hoped one of them would want to publish the magazine.

None of the publishers thought the Wallaces' idea would work. So, the Wallaces decided to sell the magazine through the mail.

The Wallaces raised enough funds to print 5,000 copies of *Reader's Digest* in 1922.

The magazine was successful. In 1926, 20,000 copies were sold by mail in the United States. By 1929, *Reader's Digest* was sold on newsstands, as well as by mail.

Reader's Digest still sells millions of copies today.

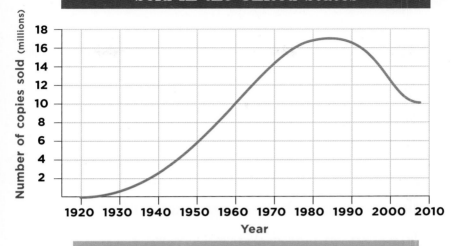

Number of Copies of *Reader's Digest* Sold in the United States

Number of copies sold (millions)

18
16
14
12
10
8
6
4
2

1920 1930 1940 1950 1960 1970 1980 1990 2000 2010

Year

In 2010, *Reader's Digest* began publishing ten times a year instead of twelve. This meant that fewer copies were published.

The Wallaces wanted to help their community. They gave money to The Juilliard School. This school in New York City teaches dance, music, and drama.

The Wallaces died in the 1980s. They left all their money to educational organizations and arts programs. *Reader's Digest* is still one of the most popular magazines in the world.

STOP AND CHECK

What problems did the Wallaces have when they started *Reader's Digest*?

Chapter 2

WHAT A PERFORMANCE!

Alvin Ailey had the idea of making dance more exciting. He wanted more people to take up dance.

Alvin was born in Texas in 1931. His father left when he was a baby, and his mother had many different jobs. When Alvin was 11, they moved to Los Angeles.

America in the 1930s

During the Great Depression in the 1930s, many banks and businesses closed. Millions of people lost their jobs and homes. Many people had no work.

Most black people couldn't get as good an education as white people. It was harder for them to get work. Many black people moved to find jobs.

In Los Angeles, Ailey became interested in dance. In the early 1950s, Ailey moved to New York City. He studied ballet, modern dance, and acting. He also worked as a dancer and actor.

Ailey formed the Alvin Ailey American Dance Theater in 1958. He wanted to use dance to help show what the African-American experience was really like.

The company's first big performance was an innovative ballet called *Blues Suite*.

Blues Suite had modern dance, jazz, ballet, and African dance.

Alvin Ailey made dance accessible to many people.

Many of Ailey's works were inspired by his childhood. His most famous dance routine is *Revelations*. It tells the story of Ailey's childhood in Texas.

Ailey was enthusiastic and caring. He started programs to teach children dance. The children also learned life skills, such as teamwork and respect. Alvin Ailey died in 1989, but his dance company is still around.

Chapter 3

HELPING "THE LITTLE FELLOWS"

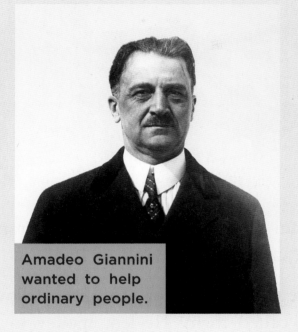

Amadeo Giannini wanted to help ordinary people.

Amadeo Giannini was a compassionate person. He started a business to help others.

Before the 1900s, only rich customers and businesses could open bank accounts and borrow money.

The banks didn't want customers who were immigrants, like Giannini's parents. They had moved from Italy to the United States in the 1860s. Giannini decided to start his own bank.

Many buildings were destroyed when an earthquake struck San Francisco in 1906.

Giannini opened his bank in San Francisco in 1904. He called it the Bank of Italy.

The new bank was for "the little fellows," as Giannini called them. He lent money to farmers, laborers, and store owners.

His undertaking was a success. Soon the bank had thousands of customers.

In 1906, an earthquake destroyed much of San Francisco. The Bank of Italy building was ruined. Giannini set up his bank out on the street. He loaned businesses money so they could rebuild after the quake.

Giannini opened more branches of the bank across California. He bought other banks as well. In 1930, he renamed all of his banks the Bank of America.

In 1932, the Bank of America gave money to help build the Golden Gate Bridge in San Francisco. The bank's money made it possible to build the bridge.

STOP AND CHECK

Why did Giannini want to start a bank?

People crossed San Francisco Bay by ferry before the Golden Gate Bridge was built.

Chapter 4

A SMART INVENTOR

Kavita Shukla was 13 when she started a business. She invented the Smart Lid to keep chemicals safe.

The lid has an alarm. It sounds when a container of chemicals is opened or leaks. Kavita got the idea when her mom forgot to screw on the gas cap after filling up the car!

Kavita's second invention came after she drank polluted water in India. Her grandmother gave her a mixture of spices so she would not get sick. It was an old remedy, and it worked.

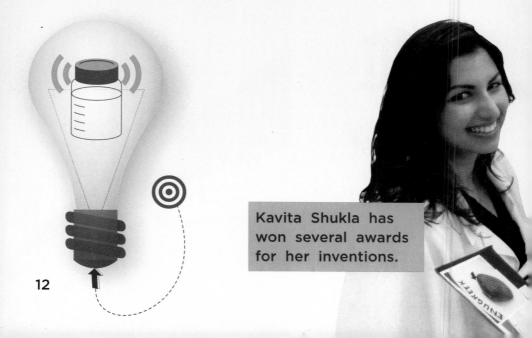

Kavita Shukla has won several awards for her inventions.

Kavita wondered if some of the spices could be used to preserve food. She found that food lasted longer if it was wrapped in paper treated with the spices. The spiced paper was also natural. It broke down in the trash.

Now Kavita runs a company that sells the paper she created. She believes her invention can help more people eat fresh food.

Start It Up

Businesses help communities by bringing jobs to an area. Businesses give their money and time to community events. Communities use the money to help people in need.

Communities must encourage businesses to start up in their areas. The businesses help communities grow. They make them better places to live.

Bill Gates started Microsoft when he was a teenager. He and his wife, Melinda, have donated about $26 billion to good causes.

You read about entrepreneurs who took big risks to start new businesses. Entrepreneurs sometimes have to borrow money from banks. They have to work hard. Some entrepreneurs give some of the money they make back to their communities.

You can look out for new ideas. You, too, could be an exceptional entrepreneur who starts small, thinks big, and helps your community.

STOP AND CHECK

What gave Kavita ideas for her inventions?

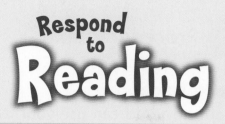

Respond to Reading

Summarize

Use important details from the selection to summarize *Start Small, Think Big*. Your graphic organizer may help.

Main Idea
Detail
Detail
Detail

Text Evidence

1. What features of a persuasive text can you find in "Start It Up" on page 13? GENRE

2. What is the main idea in Chapter 2? What are the key details that support the main idea? MAIN IDEA AND KEY DETAILS

3. The word *invention* on page 12 includes the suffix *-ion*. This suffix changes a verb into a noun. Use this information to define *invention*. SUFFIXES

4. Choose one of the entrepreneurs in *Start Small, Think Big*. Write about how the entrepreneur helped other people. Use details from the text in your answer. WRITE ABOUT READING

Compare Texts

Read about how you can use your own money to help yourself and others.

Spending and Saving

Do you spend your own money, or do you **deposit** it into a savings account?

It's fun to spend money on things you want. It's also a smart idea to save money. You may also want to save some money to help others.

Some things may take only a few weeks to save for, such as a T-shirt. Others may take months. You might want to buy a bike that costs $200. You need to do the math and make a savings plan.

You can set up a **budget**. It will help you plan how much to save and how much to spend.

Setting Up a Budget

1. List the money you get, such as your allowance or birthday money.

2. List the things that you buy every week.

3. Figure out how much you can save each week.

4. Figure out how long it will take you to reach your goal.

Money In	
Allowance	$10
Other	$8
TOTAL	**$18**
Money Out	
Corner Store	$3
Other (Game)	$10
Charity	$2
TOTAL	**$15**
MONEY SAVED = $3	

Check your budget each week to see how close you are to your goal. If you spend less, you'll reach your goal faster.

You can use your savings for all kinds of things. You might even use your money to start a small business!

Make Connections

How can making a budget help you to help others? ESSENTIAL QUESTION

Why do you think the people who started businesses in *Start Small, Think Big* used some of their money to help others? What kind of organization would you like to support with your money? TEXT TO TEXT

Glossary

budget *(BUH-jit)* a plan for spending and saving *(page 17)*

deposit *(di-POZ-it)* put money into a bank account *(page 16)*

entrepreneurs *(ahn-truh-pruh-NUHRZ)* people who start their own businesses *(page 2)*

Index

Focus on
Social Studies

Purpose To understand how a plan can help you raise money to help others

Procedure

Step 1 ▶ Choose an organization or activity in your community.

Step 2 ▶ Think about how you could raise money for the organization or activity. You might think about having a bake sale, a theme night, or a fun run. You might choose something that will go on for several weeks. Think big.

Step 3 ▶ Figure out how much money you'll need to raise to reach your goal. How much time will you need to reach it?

Step 4 ▶ Now make a plan to raise the money. What will you need to do?